AF341961

CULTURE OF LIFE
A CATHOLIC PERSPECTIVE

FATHER JOHN J. PASQUINI

Vero House
Publishing, Corp.

Culture of Life
A Catholic Perspective
by Fr. John J. Pasquini
Copyright © 2012 John J. Pasquini

Published by
Vero House Publishing, Corp.
5460 Corsica Place
Vero Beach, FL 32967.

For more information,
see www.VeroHousePublishing.com,
email admin@VeroHousePublishing.com,
or call 888-292-7160.

Paperback version printed in the United States of America.

Paperback ISBN: 978-0-9886539-2-4
Digital ISBN: 978-0-9886539-3-1

Table of Contents

Preface
Hierarchy of Values

What is it that makes one a great or holy citizen? A great and holy citizen seeks to protect and preserve the good and seeks to overturn evil. A holy citizen seeks to do what Jesus would do!

A good and holy citizen must be familiar with the Church's teachings, whether one is dealing with immigration, refugee assistance, international peace and justice, healthcare, workers' rights, conscience protection, education, the environment, the nature of marriage, parental rights, stem cell research, euthanasia, the death penalty, abortion, etc.

A wonderful place to find answers to these pressing questions is in the *Catechism of the Catholic Church*—which is the summary of the Church's consistent teachings on faith and morals as given to us by the successors of the apostles, the bishops, in union with the successor of Peter, the pope.

As we grow in humility through the sacrament of reconciliation and enter into a deep experience of Christ in the sacrament of the Eucharist—which awakens and empowers the other sacraments—we become more and more Christ-like. Prayer and the sacraments help us to see our predominant negative inclinations, faults and blind spots. Prayer, a grace-experience, helps to cure and elevate our wounded nature. We become more aware of the moral law, the moral virtues, the hierarchy of values, the theological virtues, the evangelical counsels, the gifts of the

Spirit and the life of the Beatitudes. We become aware of the temptations towards rebellion and sin—which we call concupiscence. We become aware of sin and vice, and the need for prayer—whether vocal, meditative or contemplative—and our need for Mary, the Mother of the Church, the Mother of Obedience and Perfection, the Icon of her son. To grow in holiness is to become people who live out the fullness of the Gospel as expressed and summarized in the *Our Father* and the *Beatitudes*.

Holiness, founded upon humility, the doorway to holiness, helps us recognize the competing spirits we face (the spirit of the world, the flesh, the devil, and the spirit of God). The discernment of spirits helps us to clearly see the issues we face.

Holiness fosters an informed conscience. An informed conscience entails self-examination, silent reflection and introspection. It demands one's absorption in the word of God and sacred tradition (the life of the Holy Spirit within the Church). An informed conscience is marked by the following qualities: A good end does not justify an evil means; Do unto others as you would like done unto you; "What you do the least of my brethren you do to me" (Mt. 25:40).

Having said all this, some parishioners inevitably and understandably come and ask, "Who am I to vote for when so few candidates share all of the Catholic Church's teachings?" It is here that we seek to vote according to a hierarchy of values. At the top of the list is the protection of the sanctity of human life and the human family. All other rights flow from these rights. For example, the right to "cheap or free healthcare" implies that there is someone alive to receive it! Likewise, the common good of a society implies that marriage and the family function as a school of values and morals, a school of holy citizenship. If the family implodes, so does society!

When in doubt, fear not! Christ did not leave us as orphans. He has blessed us with his life, his Church. Let us pray, reflect, study and seek to be obedient to the successors of the apostles in union with the successor of Peter, the pope. In doing so, we can be assured of our role in fulfilling the obligations of holy citizenship.

The Culture of Life, the Gospel of Life, is based on the hierarchy of values. The Culture of Death of Evil slithers its way into society when this hierarchy is denied or ignored.

The following work is a much needed guide to being in accord with the Culture of Life, a culture where a person can be in harmony with nature, his or her neighbor, and with God. It is a guide toward abundant living and a healthy culture.

Introduction
A Loving, Forgiving People

There is no love or compassion without truth, reason, or an informed conscience.

We as people of love must seek to embrace and nourish the "culture of life" amidst a "culture of death." We as people are called to promote and defend the sanctity of life from conception to natural death through a life of prayer, service, and education.

The "culture of death," under the guise of good, assaults the dignity of the person through abortion, embryonic stem-cell research, cloning, and other forms of destructive biological engineering. The dignity of the person is battered by poverty, crime, disenfranchisement, and it is shattered through the death penalty and euthanasia. The very source of a healthy society, the family, is under attack. When the dignity of the person and the family is compromised at any stage, and in any manner, a society is bound to disintegrate.

There is no love or compassion without truth, reason, or an informed conscience.

I
Personhood

If you were to ask any embryologist when life begins, you would hear without hesitation: "Life begins when a human ovum is fertilized by a human spermatozoa. That is, life begins at syngamy when a one-celled zygote is produced. At syngamy a human organism, a member of the human species, comes into existence." In other words, in terms we can understand, human life begins at conception (syngamy).

At conception we have a human organism, a human being.

Having said this, however, one may ask: "If this is so, why is it that abortion, stem-cell research on embryos, and all kinds of experimentations on embryos is permitted to take place?"

The answer to this is based, in part, upon an ancient pagan theory that is often today referred to as the theory of "delayed hominization." This theory essentially maintains that one can be a human organism without being a human person. For some scientists, ethicists, and moralists, if one is not a human person then one does not have the rights of a human person.

The great dilemma that arises from such a view is: When does one become a person? For some individuals, one becomes a person at approximately two weeks after conception when the embryo is implanted in the uterus;

for others it is at three weeks when the heart is beating, or at six weeks when brain waves are measurable and the child moves and responds to touch, or at eight weeks when the body is completely formed, or at twelve weeks when all organ systems are functioning, or at twenty weeks at viability (when the child can live outside the womb), or at birth, or at infancy, or at four to six years of age, and so on. Many, therefore, believe that if a child is born with a defect, then a mother should have the right to euthanize (kill) the child within the first two to three days of birth. Others maintain that one is not a human person until one is able to experience abstract thought and reflective self-consciousness.

This false vision of life has tragic consequences, for if one can assign personhood by an arbitrary standard, then one can take away personhood accordingly by an arbitrary standard.

In the early years of this country, slavery was justified on the grounds that slaves were considered property and not persons. In Nazi Germany the handicapped, the seriously ill, the gypsies, and finally the Jews and all who opposed Nazism were exterminated for failing to be authentic Aryan persons.

If you take a person's personhood away, you can do almost anything to a person. When one plays with a person's personhood all kinds of egregious acts are in the shadows waiting to come out.

Since many Alzheimer's patients and many mentally handicapped individuals are incapable of abstract thought and self-reflection, are they to be put to death for not being persons? Sadly to say this is occurring in many western countries!

For the Catholic, one is a human being and a human person from the moment of conception. There is no separating of the two! As Pope John Paul the Great clarified in the Gospel of Life: "How can one be a human being without being a human person?" Or as the ecclesiastical writer of the third century, Tertullian, wrote: "one becomes a human person only because one already is a human person."

At the moment of conception a person's sex, facial features, body type, hair, eye, and skin color are determined. Even a person's future intelligence and personality are influenced by the genetic code present at conception. Every aspect of who and what a person is is present from the beginning of human life with the exception of the exercise of free will, time to grow and mature, and the influences of the environment. What I am at 48 is what I was at conception with the exception of the exercise of my will, time to grow and mature, and environmental influences. Everything I will be at 67 is what I am now at 48, with the same exceptions.

From the moment of conception, we are simultaneously human beings and human persons.

Let no one take your personhood away from you or anyone else. Be vigilant, for one day they might come after you in the name of compassion.

II
Abortion through the Catholic Ages

"Do you not know that you are the temple of God,
and that the Spirit of God dwells in you?
If anyone destroys God's temple,
God will destroy that person;
for the temple of God,
which you are,
is holy."
1 Corinthians 3:16-17

Can one be a pro-choice, pro-abortion Catholic? Is such a thing possible?

The Scriptures

The Scriptures are clear regarding the sanctity of life from conception to natural death: In Genesis 25: 22-24 we read: "The children in Rebekah's womb jostled each other so much that she exclaimed, 'If this is to be so, what good will it do me!' She went to consult the Lord, and he answered her: 'Two nations are in your womb....'" In Jeremiah 1:5 we read: "Before I formed you in the womb I knew you, before you were born I dedicated you, a prophet to the nations I appointed you." In Isaiah we read: "Thus says the Lord who made you, who formed you from the womb: Fear not, O Jacob, my servant whom I have chosen" (v. 2 and v. 24). In Isaiah 49:2 we read: "The Lord called me from birth, from my mother's womb he gave me my name." In Job 10:8, 11 we read: "Your hands have formed me and fashioned me; with skin and flesh you clothed me, with bones and sinews you knit me together." In Job 31:15 we read: "Did not he who made me in the womb make him? Did not the same One fashion us before our birth?" In Psalm 139:13-16 we read: "You formed my inmost being; you knit me in my mother's womb. I praise you, so wonderfully you made me, wonderful are your works! My very self you knew; my bones were not hidden from you, when I was being made in secret, fashioned as in the depths of the earth. Your eyes foresaw my actions; in your book all are written down; my days were shaped, before one came to be." In Ecclesiastes 11:5 we read: "Just as you know not how the breath of life fashions the human frame in the mother's womb, so you know not the work of God which he is accomplishing in the universe." In Luke 1:41-44 we read, "When Elizabeth heard Mary's greeting, the infant leaped in her womb, and Elizabeth, filled with the Holy Spirit, cried out in a loud voice and said, 'Most blessed are you among women, and blessed is the fruit of your womb. And how does this happen to me that the mother of my Lord should come to me? For at the moment the sound of your greeting reached my ears, the infant in my womb leaped for joy." And in Luke 1:36 we read: "Behold, Elizabeth has conceived a son in her old age, and this is the sixth month for her..." Finally, in Revelation 9:21f we read: "Nor did they repent of their murders, their magic potions, their unchastity..." (The phrase "magic potions" is from the Greek word pharmakeia, which means, in this context, an abortion causing agent.)

Early Church Writings

In the *Didache* (ca. 65) *the Teaching of the Twelve Apostles,* we read: "You shall not kill an unborn child or murder a newborn infant" (II, 2). In Barnabas' *Epistle II* (ca. 70) we read: "You shall love your neighbor more than your own life. You shall not slay the child by abortion." In Tertullian's *Apologetics* (ca. 177) we read: "For us murder is once and for all forbidden; so even the child in the womb, while the mother's blood is still being drawn on to form the human being, it is not lawful for us to destroy. To forbid birth is only quicker murder. He is a man, who is to be a man; the fruit is always present in the seed" (197). In Athenagoras' *Legatio pro Christianis,* (ca. 177) we read: "Those who use drugs to bring about an abortion commit murder and will have to give an account to God for their abortion." In Minucius Felix's Octavius (ca. 200) we read: "There are women, who, by the use of medicinal potions, destroy the unborn life in their wombs, and murder the child before they bring it forth." In Clement of Alexandria's *Christ the Educator II* (ca. 150) we read: "If we would not kill off the human race born and developing according to God's plan, then our whole lives would be lived according to nature. Women who make use of some sort of deadly abortion drug kill not only the embryo but, together with it, all human kindness." In Augustine's *De Nuptius et Concupiscus* (354-430) we read: "Sometimes lustful cruelty or cruel lust goes so far as to seek to procure baneful sterility, and if this fails the fetus conceived in the womb is in one way or another is smothered or evacuated, in the desire to destroy the offspring before it has life, or if it already lives in the womb, to kill it before it is born." In Jerome's *Letter to Eustochium* (ca. 340-420) we read: "Some unmarried women, when they are with child through sin, practice abortion by the use of drugs. Frequently they kill themselves and are brought before the ruler of the lower world guilty of three crimes; suicide, adultery against Christ, and murder of an unborn child." In Basil the Great's *First Canonical Letter* (ca. 329-379) we read: "The hairsplitting difference between formed and unformed makes no difference to us. Whoever deliberately commits abortion is subject to the penalty for homicide."

Pope Pius XI in *Casti Connubii* argued that it is a "very grave crime [to take] the life of the offspring hidden in the mother's womb" (63). Pius XII declared in the *Declaration of Procured Abortions* that "it must in any case be clearly understood that a Christian can never conform to a law which is in itself immoral and such is the case of a law which would admit, in principle, the licity of abortion. Nor can a Christian take part in a propaganda campaign in favor of such a law, or vote for it. Moreover, he may not collaborate in its application" (#5, 22). Pope John XXIII explained in *Mater et Magistra* that "human life is sacred…from it very inception. Those who violate his laws not only offend the divine majesty and degrade themselves and humanity, they also sap the vitality of the political community of which they are members" (#194). Pope Paul VI explained that "life must be safeguarded with extreme care from conception, for abortion and infanticide are abominable crimes" (cf. *Gadium et spes*, 51). Pope John Paul II in *Evangelium Vitae* stated that "right from fertilization the adventure of a human life begins…"(#60). Pope Benedict XVI magnificently argued that abortion is not a human right, but the very opposite of it: "The fundamental human right [from conception until its natural end], the presumption of every other right, is the right to life…" (Hofburg Address, Vienna, cf. AFP 2, 7, 07).

We were created in the "image and likeness" of God" (Gen. 1:27). We are the "body of Christ" (1 Cor. 12:12f; Rom. 12:5; Eph. 1:22f) and the "Temple of God" (1 Cor. 3:9-10, 15-16). Anyone who aborts a child is aborting the "image and likeness" of God, the "body of Christ," the "temple of God." They are aborting God.

Can one be a pro-abortion, pro-choice Catholic? Is such a thing possible?

III
The Pill,
the Silent Abortion

If we were to ask most couples about the negative side effects associated with the use of the pill, most couples would have a general idea regarding these effects, either through information obtained from their doctors or from pharmacists. They may not be aware of the fifty-two side effects associated with the use of the pill, but they more than likely would be aware of the most talked about side effects such as strokes, heart attacks, and blood clots.

If, however, we were to ask most couples about the method in which the pill works in preventing the birth of children, there would be a tremendous amount of ignorance.

There are two major types of pills that are being used in preventing the birth of children: those that contain a combination of estrogen and progestogen and those that contain only progestogen. Both of these types of pills prevent the birth of children either through preventing ovulation or preventing the effective migration of sperm in the uterus, or by preventing implantation. In the *Physicians' Desk Reference* the combination pills are described as operating in the following manner: "Combination oral contraceptives act by suppression of gonadotropins. Although the primary mechanism of this action is the inhibition of ovulation, other alterations include changes in the cervical mucus (which increase the difficulty of sperm entry into the uterus) and the endometrium (which reduce the likelihood of implantation)."

In terms of the progestogen-only pill, the *Physicians' Desk Reference* states: "[Progestogen-only pills] alter cervical mucus, exert a progestational effect on the endometrium, interfering with implantation, and in some patients, suppress ovulation."

Therefore, the pill (whether the combination pill or the progestogen-only pill) has the potential for being an abortifacient—an abortion-causing agent. When conception takes place, a human being is present. The pill at this point, because it weakens the lining of the uterus, prevents this human being from being implanted in the womb of the mother.

This is a silent abortion. As the Church teaches in its documents, as in the 1994 American document *Ethical and Religious Directives for Catholic Healthcare Services* (n. 45): "Every procedure whose sole immediate effect is the termination of pregnancy before viability is an abortion, which, in its moral context, includes the interval between conception and implantation of the embryo."

What is said of the "pill" can be said, with slight variations, on all the other hormonal methods of contraception, including Norplant, Depo-Provera, RU-486 and Ovral.

Similar abortifacient effects are also apparent in the use of intrauterine devices such as Lippes Loop and the Copper-T 380A.

How many silent victims are being lost because of the unknowing actions of couples? Who is at fault for their ignorance?

Europe is experiencing a decline in its native population through a contraceptive mentality and an attachment to the "culture of death." In many European countries the death rate is overwhelming the birth rate. It is conceivable that within a few centuries the European race will be replaced by another race.

IV
Natural Family Planning

The use of contraceptives is intrinsically evil. As *Familiaris Consortio*, 32, explains regarding the evil of contraceptives and the contraceptive attitude:

> *"The innate language that expresses the total reciprocal self-giving of husband and wife is overlaid, through contraception, by an objectively contradictory language, namely, that of not giving oneself totally to the other. This leads not only to a positive refusal to be open to life but also to a falsification of the inner truth of conjugal love, which is called upon to give itself in personal totality....The difference, both anthropological and moral, between contraception and recourse to the rhythm of the cycle...involves in the final analysis two irreconcilable concepts of the human person and of human sexuality."*

The old fashioned "calendar-rhythm" method, which was highly inaccurate and inadequate, is no longer the means used for natural family planning. Today the methods of determining a woman's fertile period has become more sophisticated and accurate. Some prefer the use of the Ovulation-Billings method, others prefer the Symtpo-Thermal method.

Those who practice one of these methods of natural family planning have a less than eight percent chance of divorcing as opposed to those who use contraceptives. The divorce rate of those who use contraceptives is over sixty percent. The reasons are simple:

1. NFP methods are natural. That is, they do not hinder the natural functioning of the body but observe and respect the natural cycle of fertility and infertility. These methods respect the bodies of the spouses, encourage tenderness, and foster the necessary freedom that is at the base of authentic self-giving love.

2. It is only in total self-giving that one can fulfill the Gospel call of "two becoming one" (cf. Mark 10:6-9). Being in harmony with one's spouse can only take place for those who dedicate themselves to total self-giving, without reservation.

3. Human life and the duty of transmitting it in cooperation with God is a spiritual gift that is not limited to this life's horizons, but has its true evaluation and full significance in reference to one's eternal destiny.

Those who practice natural family planning, as opposed to artificial contraception, make the sex act a spiritual act, a unitive, bonding, and creative act.

Without God marriage is impossible, and where marriage collapses, so does the very structure of a society.

V
Post-Abortion Trauma

Trauma, if not dealt with, will manifest itself in the most negative of ways. Hence, the trauma of abortion, if not dealt with, will wreak havoc on a woman and consequently on much of society.

Women who have had abortions often seek to deal with the pain in essentially four manners: through suppression, repression, rationalization, and/or compensation (cf. Theresa Burke, Ph.D., *Forbidden Grief,* 2002).

Suppression

Women who seek to suppress the trauma of abortion consciously push away or push down any negative feelings. They do everything possible not to think about the abortion or its trauma. These are women who often turn to alcohol or drugs to numb their pain, or become workaholics to keep busy and distracted, or avoid prayer, church, and God. It is not unusual to notice a person get up and walk out of church when the very word abortion is mentioned. They are not being disrespectful. They are simply avoiding a reminder of their trauma.

In the most extreme cases, women who suppress their pain will often have more than one abortion with the hope that each abortion will lessen the trauma (forty-five percent of women who have had an abortion, will have more than one-- three to ten is not unusual). The mentality is: "The more I have, the less it will hurt."

Repression

Women who repress the trauma of abortion do so without any conscious awareness. Repression is a subconscious defense mechanism where the mind blocks out any negativity. These repressed feelings manifest themselves through an inability to bond with their husbands or children and an inability to form deep relationships.

Repression also manifests itself in certain disorders and unexplained actions. A woman went in for counseling because of a lingering depression. The woman was astonishingly beautiful with the exception of her hair. It was so short that a comb could not pass through it. After months of therapy, the mystery was uncovered. The woman's hair was so short because she could not bear to hear the sound of a hair dryer. It reminded her of the suction catheter used during her abortion. Likewise, through therapy, another woman was able to recognize that the only reason she had replaced all her carpets in her home with wood flooring was that the sound of the vacuum cleaner likewise reminded her of the suction catheter used in abortion. These women were doing things they could not explain because they were subconsciously trying to deal with the trauma of abortion. It was through therapy that what was being repressed came to light.

Rationalization

At a local abortion facility, while a group of pro-life individuals were gently and lovingly praying the Rosary, a woman volunteer from the clinic drove into the parking lot, jumped out of her car, and ran over to confront a woman praying. She was so filled with anger and malice that her body shook as she screamed.

This is a classic example of the coping mechanism of rationalization. Rationalization is an argument that one makes to justify one's action as acceptable. It is marked with intolerance, anger, and hatred. The rationalization of many women who have had an abortion is that "if it is legal, it must be okay." Therefore, any threat to the legal status of abortion is a threat to their coping with the trauma.

This is the same rationalization that is behind the efforts to eliminate the "Choose Life" plates in many states. These plates are a threat to the legal status of abortion.

Compensation

Compensation is a coping mechanism that seeks to "make up" for past mistakes. Often women feel they must be punished in order to compensate for the evil of their abortion. This manifests itself in self-mutilation, attempted suicides, anorexia, bulimia, and a wide range of self-punishing behaviors.

This compensation mechanism is often seen in what is known as the "perfect mother syndrome." Mothers often try to make up for what they did to their first child by trying to be the perfect mother for their subsequent children.

They can often become doting and controlling parents in their efforts to make everything perfect.

The reality of post-abortion trauma and its manifestation can in no way be completely described in such a short essay. Book after book has been written about this subject. My hope is simply to illustrate one small portion of the damage that is done to women in the name of abortion and so-called women's rights. The trauma that women experience after having had an abortion will take many forms and may appear immediately after the abortion or some forty years afterwards. One way or another, a woman's life will never be the same, either at a very conscious level or a subconscious level.

Women who have had an abortion experience overwhelming feelings of guilt, isolation, grief, anger, depression, and shame. They often develop obsessive compulsive disorders and various forms of addictive behaviors such as eating disorders, and alcohol and drug abuse. Women often feel alienated from God and from the Church. At times they feel anger at God and the sense that they can never be forgiven.

Let us make no mistake about it. Those who support abortion have no love for women. It is no coincidence that physicians who perform abortions have among the highest rates of reported spousal abuse.

Post-Abortion Trauma: A Family Affair

That abortion devastates women is obvious from study after study, but what is less known is that abortion also impacts fathers, surviving siblings, and grandparents. Abortion is a family tragedy.

Men, Fathers

Men are often haunted by nightmares about their unborn children. They often develop feelings of great guilt, remorse, sadness, and powerlessness. They often punish themselves by forms of self abuse such as alcoholism, drug use, or bodily mutilations (i.e., extensive piercings and tattoos). At times men can turn feelings of betrayal, powerlessness, and loss of trust into acts of aggression and abuse toward women. Men often seek to run away from these feelings by leaving their partners. It is not unusual that an abortion marks the end of a relationship.

Siblings

Siblings that become aware of their parents role in abortion are often afflicted by confusion and a general fear of the world. Siblings often suffer what is known as "Survivor Syndrome," which is a mixture of anger and guilt associated with the overwhelming feeling of "why did I survive and my brother or sister didn't?" At times siblings feel that somehow their existence has caused the death of their sibling: "Mom and Dad could only handle one of us!"

Grandparents

Grandparents often experience many of the above symptoms of post-abortion trauma, but most feel a sense of anger, bitterness, resentment, depression and despair over the abortion. Often they feel unable to forgive their daughter or step-daughter. Most often, whether at a conscious or subconscious level, grandparents experience an un-repairable strain on their relationship with their daughter or step-daughter.

Abortion is a family tragedy and a societal tragedy. The more we permit the continuance of abortion, the more the family will die out. When the family structure dies, the culture will die, and society will cease to exist as we now know it!

Those who suffer from the trauma of abortion can seek help through several healing programs provided by churches and certain psychologists and psychiatrists. Two of the most famous Catholic Post-Abortion healing ministries are Rachel's Vineyard and Project Rachel.

VI
Abortion and the
African-American Community

Abortion is the leading cause of death in the African-American community. Abortion dwarfs all the major causes of death in the African-American community (US Center for Disease Control).

Margaret Sanger, the founder of Planned Parenthood, the leading provider of abortion services in the world, wrote to a colleague, Clarence Gamble in 1939:

> *"The 'poorer areas, particularly in the South…are producing alarmingly more than their share of future generations. We do not want the word to get out that we want to exterminate the Negro population'." (Smith Collection, Smith College).*

Is it a coincidence that a disproportionate number of abortion clinics in the United States are located in minority neighborhoods? Is it a coincidence that thirty-five percent of abortions are performed on African-American women, while they only represent twelve percent of the female population (US CDC/ US Census Bureau). Is it a coincidence that more African-Americans have died from abortion than any other cause?

Planned Parenthood was founded with evil intentions, and what is founded on evil most often continues to foster evil. While many current members of Planned

Parenthood may not be racists per se, they do, however, work with an organization that in its inception systematically and deliberately sought to hinder the growth and success of any non-Caucasian race.

Human life is sacred for it "involves the creative action of God and it remains forever in a special relationship with the Creator (CCC 2258). Every human being bears the handprint of God, the image and likeness of his or her Creator. God sees and loves in us what he sees and loves in his Son, Jesus Christ. Any act that diminishes the dignity of any human person is a direct assault on God, a direct assault on his image and likeness, his very presence in the core of every human being. An act of racism is an act of hatred toward God.

Racism is a cancer that destroys the fabric of society, and abortion providers are among the leading proponents of this type of racism in the African-American community, whether they are aware of it or not.

VII
Breast Cancer and Abortion

The month of October is often the month dedicated to breast cancer awareness. Many television networks and programs place great emphasis on informing the public about the causes, treatments, and the importance of early detection.

What is astonishing is that one never hears on the networks and very rarely in the print media the scientifically well-established and well-known correlation between breast cancer and abortion.

Why is this so? What are so many people afraid of?

Breast cancer is the leading cause of cancer death in the United States for women between the ages of 29-59. Every year, approximately 180,000 women are diagnosed with breast cancer and more than 41,000 die from this disease. One out of every eight women will develop breast cancer during their lifetime (CDC, 2000).

During the past forty-three years, over seventy studies by the most prestigious universities and journals of medicine have shown a correlation between breast cancer and abortion. In the United States, thirteen out of fourteen studies of American women have implicated abortion as a risk factor for breast cancer.

Women under thirty who have had an abortion and have a family history of breast cancer increase their risk of breast cancer by eighty percent. After the age of thirty, this increases to 270 percent. Women with a family history of breast cancer and who have had two or more abortions have a 600 percent increased risk of developing breast cancer. Women younger than eighteen who have had an abortion have a 150 percent increased risk of developing breast cancer, with an 800 percent increased risk if they had their abortions between the ninth and twenty-fourth week of pregnancy (cf. *Clincial Oncology*, 1989, 1:11-18; *Am. J. Epidemiol*, 1990, 131:804-814; *Brit. Med. J.* 1990, 299:1430-1432; *Cancer* 1991, 67:1285-1290; *Int. J. Cancer*, 1991, 48:816-820; *JNCI*, 1994, 86:1584-1592; *J. Epidemiol*, 1996, 50:481-496).

The biological hypothesis for the correlation between abortion and breast cancer is still uncertain, but the American Cancer Society in 1997 proposed the following theory—oddly a theory they would eliminate from their website after 1997. Could it be that the pro-abortion forces had any influence on them? In any event, in 1997 they argued the following:

> *"Breast cells have been hypothesized to be the most susceptible to transformation into malignant cells when breast tissue contains primarily rapidly growing and undifferentiated epithelial cells—i.e., pregnancy. Some investigators have hypothesized that the termination of pregnancy in the first two trimesters may alter the carcinogenic potential of breast tissue by interrupting the complete differentiation of breast cells that occurs during full-term pregnancy and confers protection."*

Dr. Chris Kahlenborn, the author of "Breast Cancer Risk and Abortion," explains it in a simpler manner:

> *"At the beginning of pregnancy there are great increases in certain hormone levels (i.e., estrogen, progesterone, etc.) that support pregnancy. In response to these changes breast cells divide and mature into cells able to produce milk. Abortion causes an abrupt fall in hormone levels, leaving breast cells in an immature state. These immature cells can more easily become cancer cells."*

Putting an end to abortion would eliminate the number one preventable risk for breast cancer (*Chicago Tribune*, May 21, 2001).

Let us break the silence. Let us force opponents of the Gospel of Life to look into the light!

VIII
Adoption,
the Loving Choice

As long as I live I will always remember a debate that took place in my religion class when I was a Catholic schoolteacher.

The debate was over the issue of abortion. It is sad to say that although this was a Catholic school, the class was divided over the issue. Many children had been indoctrinated into the culture of death's pro-abortion stance.

I will always remember one particular boy who led the pro-abortionists in the debate. He knew every cliché and every pro-abortion argument. His father was a writer for a local daily newspaper (renowned for its anti-Catholic stands) and a pro-abortionist. The boy had learned well from his father.

The debate went back and forth for close to forty-minutes. Every possible argument on both sides of the issue had been exhausted.

At this point I made the decision to stop the debate and move on to another subject. I knew that no consensus could be found amongst students.

The class was divided into two irreconcilable visions of reality, two irreconcilable worldviews.

The culture of death and the culture of life had come face to face.

Just when I had given up all hope, the shiest little

girl in the class raised her hand. This surprised me as well as all the students.

This little girl rarely spoke up in class, yet she always attracted much attention.

The girls all wanted to be her friend and the boys all wanted to impress her. So when this girl raised her hand, the entire class was completely focused on hearing what she had to say.

I will never forget her words. She said: "When my mom was pregnant she was going to have an abortion, but she decided to put me up for adoption instead. I'm so glad she did. I have the best adoptive parents in the world. I love my parents so much and I love my life. I'm so happy I'm alive. I'm so happy I was adopted."

In all my years as a schoolteacher I never heard a class become so quiet. A pin could have dropped and the whole class would have heard it hit the ground. The debate had been won. Christ had prevailed.

Several years later I was having my car repaired at a local dealership when this girl, now a college educated, well-adjusted, joyful adult, came into the dealership hand in hand with her father.

Her smile brightened the entire room. What a wonderful gift she had become to the world, I thought.

According to the U.S. Health and Human Services, the average abortion takes five to ten minutes to perform, while the average wait to adopt a child is two to ten years. Instead of aborting one out of every four children conceived in this country, we should be saving these children in order to provide childless parents with children.

Instead of abortion, the loving choice of adoption should be the option for mothers who are unwilling or incapable of being adequate parents.

Let us not extinguish pretty smiles.

IX
Never-Ending Hope

A professor of philosophy asked his students to debate an issue. The professor stated: "What would you do given the following situation?"

There was a man who was born into a poor family where his distant alcoholic father would beat him on a nightly basis. He lived in a hostile and abusive home environment.

In adulthood, he suffered from bouts of depression, irritability, panic, and various disorders. He suffered from bouts of chronic abdominal pain and colic, diarrhea, nausea, thoracic gout, poor digestion, rheumatism, deafness, alcoholism and possibly syphilis.

He was a complete failure in love and in his relationships.

"Given what you know," the professor continued, "would it have been better for this person to never have been born?"

The overwhelming answer came back, "Yes. No one should have to live such a life."

The professor stared at the students and quietly responded: "You have just killed Beethoven!"

How many Beethoven's have we killed? How many Pius Xs, John Paul IIs, Martin Luther Kings, Gandhis, Mother Teresas of Calcutta, George Washingtons, Abraham Lincolns, Michelangelos, Raphaels, Shakespeares, Dantes, and so forth, have been aborted? How many religious leaders, presidents, world leaders, discoverers, scientists, doctors, teachers have been aborted?

Would there still be cancer in the world? Would there still be heart disease? What about diabetes, Parkinson's, Alzheimer's, schizophrenia, depression, pneumonia, influenza, cerebral palsy, hepatitis, HIV, AIDS, kidney and liver decease? Have we killed the person or persons who would have cured these diseases?

Pope John Paul the Great reminded every country that supported abortion: "A culture that allows for abortion is a culture that is bound to disintegrate." Abortion extinguishes hope!

X
Embryonic Stem Cell Research: Hindering Moral Scientific Advancement

Stem cells are cells that have not undergone maturation and theoretically can become any of the 220 cell types and any of the 210 specialized tissue types that make up the human body.

Because stem cells are like "blank slates," they theoretically can morph into any kind of human tissue. They theoretically can become replacement parts for unhealthy cells and tissues. The benefits from stem cell research provides the future with great possibilities in the cure and treatment of illnesses such as Parkinson's, Alzheimer's, heart disease, and diabetes.

Stem cells can be obtained immorally by the destruction of human life (i.e., human embryos) or they can be obtained morally from adults in a safe manner (i.e., from muscles, umbilical cords, bone marrow, the placenta, and from a wide variety of other adult tissues).

The media and Hollywood stars have embraced the immoral use of embryonic stem cell research with a passion and have completely ignored the morally acceptable use of stem cells acquired through moral means.

Immorally obtained embryonic stem cells have never helped a human patient (NCCB, Life Issue Forum, 2001; *Science,* April, 2001). During the National Academy of Sciences' workshop on "Stem Cells and the Future of

Regenerative Medicine" held in Washington, D.C., Marcus Grompe, M.D., Ph.D., an expert in molecular and medical genetics, stated: "There is no evidence of therapeutic benefit from embryonic stem cells," and Dr. Bert Vogelstein, chairman of John Hopkins University's Institute of Medicine studying stem cell research pointed out that any therapeutic claim of benefit from embryonic stem cell research is purely "conjectural."

On the other hand, great success has been attained in the use of adult stem cells. Adult stem cells not only have a future in curing and treating illnesses, they are doing so right now. Adult stem cells are currently being used in the treatment of multiple sclerosis, lupus, rheumatoid arthritis, stroke, anemia, Epstein-Barr virus infection, cornea damage, blood and liver diseases, brain tumors, retinoblastoma, ovarian cancer, solid tumors, testicular cancer, leukemia, breast cancer, neuroblastoma, non-Hodgkins' lymphoma, renal cell carcinoma, diabetes, heart damage; as well as cartilage, bone, muscle, and spinal-cord damage (NCCB, Life Issue Forum, 2001; *Science,* April, 2001; *Lancet,* January 2001; APR, 2000).

Given the benefits of adult stem cells, the question must be asked: Why are so many individuals preoccupied with embryonic stem cell research which involves the destruction of human life? Given the success of adult stem cells, you would think that these individuals would want improved funding and research in the field of adult stem cell experimentation.

The media and Hollywood's preoccupation with embryonic stem cells is an assault on the dignity of human life and a hindrance to the advancement of sound, moral science.

When life is of little value, the potential for grave immorality is just around the corner!

XI
Human Cloning:
Playing God

*"We are going to be one with God.
We are going to have
almost as much knowledge
and almost as much power as God"*
Richard Sheed
(National Public Radio, 98)

In theory, human cloning is a way of producing a genetic replica of a person without sexual reproduction.

Cloning occurs when the nuclear material from a cell of an organism's body (a somatic cell) is transplanted into a female reproductive cell (an oocyte) whose nuclear material has been removed or inactivated in order to produce a new, genetically identical organism.

Those who favor cloning argue that one could theoretically harvest cells, blood, tissues, and much needed organs such as hearts, livers and kidneys for therapeutic use.

These harvested "products" would be considered ideal for they would be immunologically matched—that is, they would eliminate the need for life-long immuno-suppressive therapy (Ahmann, NCBQ, 2001).

At another level, cloning would provide a means for sterile couples to reproduce.

At a glance cloning may appear appealing to some but in reality it is radically evil. As the ethicist Hans Jonas has written, [human cloning] is the most despotic…and the most slavish form of genetic manipulation" (*Tecnica, medicina edetica,* 1997).

The *Pontificia Academia Pro Vita* in its "Reflections on Cloning" points out that human cloning would radically damage the meaning, rationality, and complimentarity of human reproduction:

- *The unitive, bonding aspect of human sexual reproduction would be lost in cloning. The precious gift of sexual intercourse as a physical and spiritual act between a man and a woman would become non-existent. A woman in theory could take the nuclear material from a somatic cell from her body and fuse it into her own ovum and produce a genetic reproduction of herself without any need of a husband.*

- *The naturally occurring balance between the male and female sex in society as well as the natural structure of the family would inevitably become distorted. As the document "Reflections on Cloning" explains: It is conceivable that "a woman could [end up being] the twin sister of her mother, lack a biological father and be the daughter of her grandfather."*

- *Human life would become viewed more as a "product," an object to be harvested, rather than as a gift of love. Cloning would suppress personal identity and subjectivity at the cost of biological qualities that could be appraised and selected. Women would be exploited for their ova and their wombs, being seen simply in terms of their "purely biological functions."*

• *Cloning could lead to a loss of genetic variation in society, thereby making society vulnerable to catastrophic illnesses and genetic defects. Naturally occurring mutations would not be sufficient to assure genetic variation.*

• *Cloning would lead to a wide array of psychological problems, whereby one would be troubled by questions such as: Who is my father? Who is my mother? Do I even have a father and mother? Who am I? What am I? Where do I come from?*

• *Cloning could lead to even greater trauma in the lives of parents who have lost a beloved child. The assumption from some heartbroken parents would be that if they could only clone their dead child, they would somehow have him or her back again. But this is not the case. A cloned individual would have a different soul and a different cultural and environmental upbringing. This child would not be what they desired or intended.*

• *One's "quality of life" would become a surrogate for one's search for meaning and salvation. A culture that is already self-centered and selfish would become even more so. It would become even more an "I, me, mine" culture."*

• *Human cloning could be the ultimate expression of narcissism and hedonism. One could envision a world that desires to clone only the so-called "beautiful" people. And who determines who are the beautiful people? In God's eyes we are all beautiful. Furthermore, one could envision a society in which a self-absorbed person would clone himself or herself so as to have spare parts in the event of illnesses.*

• *And finally, but most importantly, cloning would assault the dignity of human life in the most cruel and exploitative way imaginable by making cloned children the subject of experiments and by preventing their births. Dr. Ian Wilmut was only capable of producing Dolly, the cloned sheep, after 277 attempts at cloning. In terms of human beings no culture could morally sustain itself by killing 277 human embryos with the hope of one surviving, nor allow for the current rate of 95 to 99 percent of embryos to die in the process of cloning.*

Richard Sheed's words echo ominously: "We are going to become one with God. We are going to have almost as much knowledge and almost as much power as God." Cloning is an experiment in playing God. And we all know what happened in the story of Adam and Eve when they attempted to play God.

Let us not make the same mistake.

XII
Genetic Engineering
Assisted Reproduction
Scientific Research on People

Scientific and medical experiments on human individuals can have great benefits for the healing of the sick. However, any forms of experimentation or science which conflicts with the dignity of the human person and the moral law are to be prohibited.

As the *Catechism of the Catholic Church* states: *"Basic scientific research, as well as applied research, is a significant expression of man's dominion over creation. Science and technology are precious resources when placed at the service of man and promote his integral development for the benefit of all. By themselves however they cannot disclose the meaning of existence and of human progress. Science and technology are ordered to man, from whom they take their origin and development; hence they find in the person and in his moral values both evidence of their purpose and awareness of their limits (2293)."*

"It is an illusion to claim moral neutrality in scientific research and its applications. On the other hand, guiding principles cannot be

inferred from simple technical efficiency, or from the usefulness accruing to some at the expense of others or, even worse, from prevailing ideologies. Science and technology by their very nature require unconditional respect for fundamental moral criteria. They must be at the service of the human person, of his inalienable rights, of his true and integral good, in conformity with the plan and the will of God (CCC 2294)."

Organ Transplants and Donations

Organ transplants are accepted as long as they conform to the moral law; that is, as long as "the physical and psychological dangers and risks to the donor are proportionate to the good that is sought for the recipient" CCC 2296).

Organ donation after death is a holy, noble, and meritorious act of love and solidarity with one's fellow human being, and is in no way contrary to the moral law.

One cannot resort, however, to the disabling mutilation of the body or the death of a human person in order to obtain an organ or organs.

At the heart of organ transplants and donations is the requirement of consent. If the donor's organ or organs are removed without his or her consent, or the consent of a legitimate proxy, then the removal of any organ or organs is an infringement on the dignity of the human body.

Autopsies

Autopsies are permitted for legal inquests and the good of scientific research as long as the body is treated with respect and charity.

Artificial Insemination

Scientific research that aims at eliminating or overcoming sterility is of great merit as long as it seeks to maintain the unitive and procreative dimensions of the sexual act.

It is gravely immoral to separate a husband from his wife (and vice versa) by introducing a third person into the reproductive process.

Donum Vitae II, 1, 5, 4 states:

"Techniques that entail the dissociation of husband and wife, by the intrusion of a person other than the couple (donation of sperm, or ovum, surrogate uterus), are gravely immoral. These techniques (heterologous artificial insemination and fertilization) infringe the child's right to be born of a father and mother known to him and bound to each other by marriage. They betray the spouses' right to become a father and a mother only through each other."

"Techniques involving only the married couple (homologous artificial insemination and fertilization) are perhaps less reprehensible, yet remain morally unacceptable. They dissociate the sexual act from the procreative act. The act which brings the child into existence is no longer an act by which two persons give themselves to one another, but one that 'entrusts the life and identity of the embryo into the power of doctors and biologists and establishes the domination of

technology over the origin and destiny of the human person. Such a relationship of domination is in itself contrary to the dignity and equality that must be common to parents and children.' Under the moral aspect procreation is deprived of its proper perfection when it is not willed as the fruit of the conjugal act, that is to say, of the specific act of the spouses' union... Only respect for the link between the meanings of the conjugal act and respect for the unity of the human being make possible procreation in conformity with the dignity of the person."

At the heart of Catholic sexuality is the inseparable bond between the unitive and procreative dimensions of the conjugal act.

These teachings can be a tremendous cross upon a couple that so much desires the gift of children. It must be remembered that children are gifts from God; they are not property that is owed to a couple. No one has a "right to a child." The child is the one that has rights in this situation, the right "to be the fruit of the specific act of the conjugal love of his parents," and "the right to be respected as a person from the moment of conception" (cf. CCC 2378; CDF, *Donum Vitae* II, 8).

For those who are unable to have children by moral means, they are encouraged to unite themselves to the sufferings of Christ, to become generative by their works of charity, and to seek the alternative of adoption, the giving a loving home for parentless children, children hungering for the love of parents.

Designer Babies

When one is able to clone or to select what sex, hair or eye color, intellect, body structure, and so forth by genetic engineering and the manipulation and choice of embryos one is going down a dangerous path. Huge distortions in the gene pool—which is essential for a healthy population—and huge distortions in the balance of the sexes in the population are bound to occur—cultures that prefer male children (often poor countries) will be over-populated with males and cultures that favor female children will lead to an overpopulation in females. Designer babies will lead to distorted populations susceptible to grave illnesses, because of the diminished gene pool and the imbalance of the sexes.

The striking, unique and unrepeatable qualities that make each of us special and distinctively beautiful are at stake when a culture seeks to play God. A culture that flirts with manipulating the origins of life is a culture flirting with extinction.

> *"Certain attempts to influence chromosomic or genetic inheritance are not therapeutic but are aimed at producing human beings selected according to sex or other predetermined qualities. Such manipulations are contrary to the personal dignity of the human being and his integrity and identity which are unique and unrepeatable"* (Donum Vitae I, 6).

Hybridization

Hybridization is the combining of two species artificially or naturally so as to form a new species. Hybridization is common in agriculture and even in animals. For example, the hybrid of a horse and a donkey is a mule. The hybrid of a lion and a tiger is a liger.

In a culture without limits, where God is the self, it is just a matter of time before scientists attempt to hybridize higher forms of life. Rumors have existed regarding attempts to hybridize chimpanzees with humans.

It is quite possible that the future will be inhabited with hybridized humanoids-- half human, half something else! The making of all forms of distorted human-like species will wreak havoc on our culture and lead to its genetic disintegration.

Prenatal Diagnosis

Prenatal diagnosis can be used as a tool for protecting the integrity of an unborn child. It provides physicians with the ability to take care of and heal unborn children, even by means of performing surgical procedures within a mother's womb. As *Donum Vitae* I, 2 indicates, prenatal diagnosis is morally licit:

> *"if it respects the life and integrity of the embryo and the human fetus and is directed toward its safeguarding or healing as an individual.... It is gravely opposed to the moral law when this is done with the thought of possibly inducing an abortion, depending upon the results: a diagnosis must not be the equivalent of a death sentence."*

Prenatal Surgery

Prenatal surgery is a powerful gift as long as the surgery is directed toward the healing and care of the child and does not involve disproportionate risks.

> *"One must hold as licit procedures carried out on the human embryo which respect the life and integrity of the embryo and do not involve disproportionate risks for it, but are directed toward its healing, the improvement of its condition of health, or its individual survival" (Donum Vitae, I, 3).*

An Often Overlooked Reality of Cloning, Embryonic Stem Cell Research, and Invitro-Fertilization

One of the often overlooked evils associated with the above practices is that in the process of cloning, or doing embryonic stem cell research, or attempting to have a child by means of artificial insemination, embryos are exploited and killed during the process—often in astronomical proportions. And it is for this reason the Church states that "it is immoral to produce human embryos intended for exploitation and as disposable biological material" (*Donum Vitae* I, 5).

Failure to respect the dignity of the human person from conception to natural death ultimately leads to the disintegration and death of a culture.

XIII
Euthanasia
Versus
Palliative Care

"I have had lots of patients
who wanted to commit suicide,
but you don't help them do it.
You learn why patients don't want to live anymore.
If they're in pain,
you give them more or better medication.
If they have trouble with their families,
you help them get the problem solved."
Elizabeth Kubler-Ross

Elizabeth Kubler-Ross was a world-renowned medical doctor and psychiatrist. She did much research and wrote several books and articles in the area of death and dying. In her research, she found that people who face death often experience episodes of denial, anger, bargaining with God, and depression. Most importantly, she pointed out that if a patient was lovingly cared for, the patient's last moments would be ones filled with acceptance and even hope.

Direct euthanasia consists in the murdering of the handicapped, the ill, and the dying—with or without their consent and knowledge—and is thus morally unacceptable (CCC 2277). In the definition used by the Congregation for the Doctrine of the Faith in its *Declaration on Euthanasia* we read: "By euthanasia is understood an action or omission of an action which of itself or by intention causes death in order that all suffering may be eliminated" (CDF, 1980a). And in *Evangelium Vitae* we read from the Holy Father that "Euthanasia is a violation of the law of God, since it is the deliberate and morally unacceptable killing of a person" (n. 65).

Today, too many terminally ill patients are being euthanized before they have come to a stage of acceptance and peace. Too many people are being put to death in times of anger, loneliness, and depression. A great injustice is being done to such people, all in the name of compassion.

The Church in its respect for the dignity of human life, and in its respect for God as the living Creator, promotes a holy death, a holy "letting go" which is filled with acceptance, peace, and hope on the part of the person entering into eternity.

The Church supports palliative care; that is, a form of care which seeks to eliminate pain and understands the redemptive value of unavoidable suffering (CCC 2279; cf. Col. 1:24). The Church therefore strongly encourages the use of painkillers in alleviating suffering, for at no stage is the "ordinary care owed to a sick person...[to be] interrupted" (CCC 2279). And for whatever pain remains, the Church encourages one to unite that suffering with Christ's for the good of one's soul and the souls of those in purgatory.

My uncle died at the young age of fifty-eight from terminal cancer. He received the best of palliative care. He died a peaceful, joyous and holy death in the arms of his loving family. Let no one deprive us of this!

XIV
Letting Go:
Discontinuing Medical Procedures

Prolonging life at all cost has never been part of the Catholic tradition (NCCB, 1986). There are times when one must let go and allow oneself or a loved one to enter into eternity.

In the Congregation for the Doctrine of the Faith's document *Donum Vitae* we read: "Discontinuing medical procedures that are burdensome, dangerous, extraordinary, or disproportionate to the expected outcome can be legitimate; it is the refusal of "over-zealous" treatment. Here one does not will to cause death (as in the case of euthanasia); one's inability to impede it is merely accepted."

Pope John Paul II in *Evangelium Vitae* writes: "When death is clearly imminent and inevitable, one can in conscience refuse forms of treatment that would only secure a precarious and burdensome prolongation of life, so long as the normal care of the sick person in similar cases is not interrupted" (CCC 2278).

The normal care of the person consists of prolonging life by ordinary means as opposed to extraordinary means. To put it more succinctly, the ordinary and obligatory means of prolonging life involve "all medicines, treatments, and operations which offer a reasonable hope of benefit for the patient and which can be obtained or used without excessive expense, pain, or burden" (Pius XII, *Discourse on Doctors*, 1957).

This is often understood to mean that proper nutrition (including intravenous feeding) and hydration are not to be withheld. In the U.S. National Conference of Bishops' *Ethical and Religious Directives*, directive 58 explains: "There should be a presumption in favor of providing nutrition and hydration to all patients, including patients who require medically assisted nutrition and hydration, as long as this is of sufficient benefit to outweigh the burdens involved to the patient."

In terms of those means of treatment which can be discontinued, Pius XII argues: "All medicines, treatments, and operations, which cannot be used or obtained without excessive expense, pain, or other burden [can be refused]." In other terms, when therapy will not benefit the person, "letting go" is ethically justifiable. To disconnect a respirator when a person has reached the point of no return is ethically acceptable and appropriate—as in the case of those who are "brain dead."

The decision to let go is ideally made in an environment where the doctor, the priest, and the family come together to pray and say, "We are here for you." It is a time where one prepares the person for eternity through the sacrament of the sick and if possible viaticum, the Eucharist for the journey. It is a time when one is aware that life never truly ends, but only changes. It is the recognition that just as a person loved you and prayed for you on his or her earthly journey, he or she will be loving you and praying for you in the presence of almighty God. "Letting go" is not the end, but the beginning of a new phase of eternal life.

XV
The Death Penalty:
Yesterday and Today

Punishment for criminal offenses has traditionally emphasized the importance of justice, retribution, deterrence and the protection of society. In terms of the death penalty, the key principle has always been the protection of society.

In describing the Church's position on the death penalty, the *Catechism of the Catholic Church* explains: "If nonlethal means are sufficient to defend and protect people's safety from the aggressor, authority will limit itself to such means, as these are more in keeping with the concrete conditions of the common good and more in conformity with the dignity of the human person" (CCC 2267).

Many people who read this passage often scratch their heads while saying: "How can this be? Isn't this the Church that has affirmed and often promoted the death penalty for centuries? What is going on?"

At first glance there may appear to be an inconsistency in the Church's current teaching on the death penalty, but in reality the Church's teaching has remained absolutely consistent.

The change in the Church's position is not due to a change in the theology as much as to developments in the ways of protecting and defending the common good of society.

Prior to the nineteenth century, violently dangerous

criminals were dealt with by means of execution or exile (which was essentially another form of capital punishment due to the atrociously harsh conditions associated with it).

The infrastructure of society prior to the nineteenth century was incapable of dealing with long-term incarceration; hence, those who posed a serious threat to society, such as the criminally insane, needed to be taken out of society for the protection of the common good, and the only means available, for all practical purposes, during this period in history was the death penalty (Ives, *A History of Penal Methods*).

By the late nineteenth century and early twentieth century, developments in the structure and organization of society as well as enlightened thought led to the possibility of incarcerating individuals for life, thereby eliminating the moral justification for the death penalty. As Pope John Paul II explains in *Evangelium Vitae*: "Today… as a result of steady improvements in the organization of the penal system [the justification for the death penalty is] practically non-existent."

Justice without mercy is cruelty. Christian justice demands that we be protected from violent criminals, and Christian mercy demands that we forgive the unforgivable and hope for the hopeless. As long as there is life, there is the possibility for repentance and conversion. There is always hope. Death extinguishes hope and any possibility of conversion. If Jesus would not pull the switch or inject a person with heart stopping chemicals, why should we? Let society imprison the dangerously uncontrollable for the remainder of their lives, and let people of faith pray for their conversion. Let us remember that "whoever brings back a sinner from the error of his way will save his soul from death and will cover a multitude of sins," and let us also remember that there is "more joy in heaven over one sinner who repents than over ninety-nine righteous persons who need no repentance" (Jms. 5:20; 5:7).

In a modern, civilized society, the death penalty has no place.

XVI
Legitimate War

Terrorism is a new way of waging war. The first impulse that engulfs us as human beings during terrorist attacks is the desire for revenge and retribution. But we as Christians, in times of difficulty, are called to calm down and allow the Spirit to enlighten us so as to act in a way that is in conformity with Christ and his Church.

In a spirit of prudence, the Church affirms the legitimate right to self-defense and war: "The legitimate defense of persons and societies is not an exception to the prohibition against the murder of the innocent that constitutes intentional killing" (CCC 2263). "Legitimate defense can be not only a right but a grave duty for someone responsible for another's life, the common good of the family or the state" (CCC 2265). "Governments cannot be denied the right of lawful self-defense, once all peace efforts have failed" (GS 79,4). In fact, governments are often called to war for the betterment and the good of the world.

Recourse to war is permissible when the following conditions are met (2309; 2313-2314; ST II-II, 64,7):

1. The cause must be just.
2. All means of avoiding war or ending aggression must be seen to be "impractical and ineffective."
3. There must be an adequate prospect for success in putting an end to the aggression or evil.

4.   The use of weaponry must be used with prudence. They must not "produce evils and disorders graver than the evil to be eliminated."

5.   Every act of self-defense or war that is aimed at the indiscriminate destruction of whole cities is prohibited. Non-combatants must never be targeted.

Acts of terrorism remind us of the challenge of peace that we as Catholics are faced with. Hostilities, excessive economic inequalities, contempt and distrust for persons, and unbending ideologies are all part of the injustices that ferment war. What is needed is a spiritual renewal throughout the world, a renewal that fosters solidarity and a sense of universal cooperation among nations. All nations are called to a spirit of brotherhood and a desire for a universal common good. Social structures, attitudes, and hearts must change (GS 83-90). Unless we take up this challenge for peace, the world will inevitably enter a new dark age. Recent events have pointed to this sad reality.

XVII
Gay Marriages/Unions:
A Pro-life Issue

Many might be tempted to say, "What in the world does homosexual activity have to do with the Pro-life movement and the "culture of life?" The answer is quite simple. When the sanctity of the sexual act is lost, then the structure of the family and society is doomed.

The Catholic Church basing "itself on Sacred Scripture, which presents homosexual acts as acts of grave depravity, [and] tradition has always declared that homosexual acts are intrinsically disordered" (CCC 2357; CDF, *Persona Humana*, 8). "They are contrary to the natural law. They close the sexual act to the gift of life. They do not proceed from genuine affective and sexual complementarity. Under no circumstances can they be approved" (CCC 2357).

Scripture is clear. The story of Sodom and Gomorrah in Genesis 19:1-14, while often argued as an account of inhospitality, is an account of the evil of homosexual activity; otherwise, why would all generations call those who perform homosexual acts sodomites? Furthermore, why would God destroy an entire city with fire and brimstone for simply failing to be hospitable? Leviticus 18:22 states: "You shall not lie with a man as with a woman; such a thing is an abomination."

Now some like to argue that there are many things forbidden by the Hebrew Scriptures which are no longer held by Christians. There are those laws which Jesus specifically addressed, as in the case of what to do with those caught in adultery (Jn. 8:3f) or in the case of those suffering from leprosy (Lk. 5:13). There is the example of eliminating the laws of circumcisions by the Apostles empowered by Christ and the Spirit (Acts 15). There is the making of all that was once "unclean" clean in Peter's revelation (Acts 10:9-33). Unless Jesus and his Church specifically clarified and overturned certain Hebraic laws, the laws were to remain. Leviticus forbids sex with your mother (18:7), with your sister (18:9), and with your aunt (18:14). It forbids bestiality (18:23) and orgies (18:23). Clearly, these things are still abominations!

But let us look at the New Testament writings written after the death and resurrection of Christ, when the Spirit of truth (Jn. 15:26; 16:13) was to be sent to the Christian community. Furthermore, let us never forget the promises of Christ, the promise that the gates of hell would not prevail against his Church (Mt. 16:18f; Jn. 16:13; 28:20; 1 Tim. 3:15) and the promise that he would be with his Church till the end of time (Jn. 20:29) by sending us the Spirit of Truth.

Let us remember that the letters to Timothy, to the Romans, and to the Corinthians in the Bible were written by Christ's greatest theologian, Paul, who lived after the resurrection of Jesus! If it wasn't for Paul, we would know very little about Christ, his Church, and Christianity in general!

In 1 Corinthians 6:9-10 we read: "Do not be deceived; neither fornicators or idolaters nor adulterers nor boy prostitutes nor sodomites…will inherit the kingdom of God." In Romans 1:26-27 the Scriptures declare: "Their females exchanged natural relations for unnatural, and the males likewise gave up natural relations with females and burned with lust for one another. Males did shameful things with males and thus received in their own persons the due penalty for their perversity." In 1 Timothy 1:10-11 we read: The "law is meant not for a righteous person but for the lawless and unruly, the godless and sinful, the unholy and profane, those who killed their fathers and mothers, murderers, the unchaste, sodomites, kidnappers, liars, perjurers, and whatever else is opposed to sound teaching, according to the glorious gospel of the blessed God, with which I have been entrusted."

It is not simply individual quotes that condemn homosexual acts, the very theology of the Old and New Testaments condemn it. The underlying theology of God's love for his people in the Old and New Testament is based on the complementarity of the sexes and on the natural law which underlies this complimentarity. Men and women are physically and psychologically different, and it is in this distinction that the complementarity between a man and a woman make the possibility of two becoming one (cf. Mt. 19:3-6; Mk. 10:6-9). The theology of Genesis and the entire Pentateuch, the theology of the Wisdom and Prophetic books of the Bible are all based on the underlying theology of the love of God for his people in the form of the love of a man for a woman in their distinct natures. In fact, there is no way of understanding the Scriptures without understanding the relationship between the sexes!

Tradition is clear. In the *Didache, The Teaching of the Twelve Apostles,* written anywhere from 65 AD to 120 AD we are told to "not be sexually perverted by committing sodomy" (cf. 4). In Polycarp's *Letter to the Philippians,* the disciple of the apostle John, we read: "Sodomites shall not inherit the Kingdom of God." And in Barnabas, often attributed as the same Barnabas who was the companion of Paul, we read: "Thou shall not commit sodomy" (n. 19). Other Fathers of the Church who have condemned homosexual acts include the following Apostolic Fathers—those who knew the apostles: Clement of Rome (ca. 88-97), a friend of the apostles Peter and Paul and ordained by them; Ignatius of Antioch (martyred in 107), a convert of the apostle John and consecrated bishop of Antioch by the apostle Peter and Paul; Papias (ca. 67-140), disciple of Polycarp and an "acquaintance of the apostles"; Hermas (ca. d. 155) of Romans 16:14.

In terms of the post-apostolic Fathers the following condemned homosexual acts: Caius, Presbyter of Rome (ca. 198); Dionysius of Corinth (ca. 166); Quadratus (ca. 125); Aristedes of Athens (ca. 140); Justin Martyr (ca. 100); Taitian (ca. 165); Athenagoras of Athens (ca. 180); Theophilus of Antioch (ca. 185); Melito of Sardis (ca. 171); Polycrates of Ephesus (ca. 125); Irenaeus of Lyon (ca. 140); Minucius Felix (ca. 218); Tertullian (ca. 155); Clement of Alexandria (ca. 150); Origen (ca. 185); Cornelius (ca. 251); Cyprian of Carthage (ca. 258); Firmilian of Caesarea (ca. 268), and so forth.

Philosophy likewise is clear. To put it bluntly a male's genitals were not created for another male, and a male's sexual organ certainly has no place in any male body! The male and female organs are complementary, just as the psychological distinctions between males and females are complementary. The homosexual act is a sex act which is contrary to the act's purpose and completely closed off to life.

Because of the nature of males and females, the sexual act is unitive and procreative. Homosexual acts are neither unitive nor procreative, and thus are a direct attack on the dignity of the sanctity of the sexual act.

In the name of acceptance and compassion, in the name of political correctness, in the name of all that is secular, same sex marriages and the homosexual lifestyle has become the flagship of the secular vision of the world. The essence of man and woman, their complimentarity, and the very nature of the natural law have been thrown away.

And what can be said about this acceptance and so called compassion? Homosexuals are fourteen times more likely to attempt suicide and three and a half more times to be successful in committing suicide than the rest of the population (Crisis 18, 1997, 24-34). An uncountable number of studies have pointed out that homosexuals have a much higher rate of interpersonal maladjustment, depression, childhood abuse, domestic violence, alcohol or drug abuse, anxiety, and other psychiatric disorders (*Archives of General Psychiatry* 56, 1999, 876-880). They have among the highest rates of drug use, including cocaine, marijuana, LSD, barbiturates, and amyl nitrate (*Journal of Gay and Lesbian Association* 4, no. 3, 2000, 101-51).

Homosexuals are prone to promiscuity. A San Francisco study by Bell and Weinberg in *Homosexualities: A Study of Diversity Among Men and Women* points out that forty-three percent of male homosexuals have more than 500 partners per year. Seventy-nine percent of their sexual activity will have been with complete strangers (Ibid.). Only three percent of male homosexuals have fewer than ten sexual partners. In terms of female homosexuals, they are less promiscuous than male homosexuals, but more promiscuous than female heterosexuals. Forty-two percent of female homosexuals have more than ten sexual partners per year, mostly with strangers (Ibid.).

Homosexuals themselves have recognized that under the best of conditions "fidelity" for them does not mean monogamy, but rather restrained promiscuity (Kurtz, New Republic, Sept. 2000, 35-41).

Male homosexuals are prone to certain cancers (especially anal cancer and genital cancers) and various diseases such as urethritis, laryngitis, prostatitis, hepatitis A and B, syphilis, gonorrhea, chlamydia, herpes, parasites, and genital warts. This is due primarily to the practice of sodomy. Since the rectum is not designed for sex, it is very fragile and subject to tearing and bleeding, thereby making the transmission of diseases easier. Homosexuals are prone to Gay Bowel Syndrome. Gay Bowel Syndrome is a clinical description for the unusual frequency of ano-rectal and colon diseases (www.conservapedia.com/Mental_Health_and_Homosexuality; "Complications of Homosexuality," *Proceedings of the Royal Society of Medicine*, (1077), vol. 55)).

In the name of compassion and love, secularists promote the cruelest of tortures on human beings! And what happens to these tortured individuals? They infect society with their angst and the false illusion of a healthy "alternative lifestyle."

Only in a society that worships utilitarianism, hedonism and ethical relativity can such a harmful lifestyle be accepted as good.

During the period of the early Church, the distinction between homosexual activity and homosexual orientation was not made, being that it was so closely associated with paganism. It is only with the Church's correct interpretation, guided by the Holy Spirit, that the distinction between orientation and activity was made. The Church makes it clear that a person's orientation is not sinful. As the *Catechism* explains: Homosexuals "must be accepted with respect, compassion, and sensitivity. Every sign of unjust discrimination in their regard should be avoided. These persons are called to fulfill God's will in their lives and, if they are Christians, to unite to the sacrifice of the Lord's Cross the difficulties they may encounter from their condition" (CCC 2358). The *Catechism* goes on to say: "Homosexual persons are called to chastity. By virtue of self-mastery that teach them inner freedom, at times by the support of disinterested friendship, by prayer and sacramental grace, they can and should gradually and resolutely approach Christian perfection" (2359).

XVIII
Divorce

Children of two parent families are statistically healthier, physically and mentally, than children of divorced parents or children from single parent homes. They have great advantages in mental health, happiness, life expectancy, and career success. They are more likely to have a happy marriage and a happy family (cf. Waite and Gallagher, *The Case for Marriage*).

Even children who live in an unhappy marriage do better than children that live in a divorced arrangement. Statistics point that even parents that fight often have happier and healthier children than divorced parents (*Journal of Adolescent Research* 1, 1986: 389-97).

Children of divorced parents get less education, are less successful in adulthood, are more prone to drugs, premarital sex, illicit pregnancy, and getting divorced themselves when they marry. Children of divorce parents tend to be more reckless and prone to accidents (*The Case for Marriage*, 129-140).

Remarriage does not improve things for children; in fact, in some cases it worsens the situation. Children who live in homes where a second marriage has taken place are dozens of times more likely to be the victims of violence and sexual abuse and they tend to live a far less healthy, happy, and stable life (*Child Abuse and Neglect* 8, 1984: 15-22; *Journal of the American Academy of Child and Adolescent Psychiatry* 20, no. 3, May 1991:358-9).

To make things worse, seventy percent of second marriages, eighty-seven percent of third marriages, and ninety three percent of fourth marriages break up within five years (*All About Families*, April 26, 2000, 1-2).

Young boys are particularly affected by divorce. Seeing one's mother with another man can leave traumatic scars. Often these children grow up resenting women as being "cheap" or promiscuous. This not only devastates relationships but society in general.

XIX
Child Abuse

Society bears the scars of the abuse of children. Two out of every three prisoners convicted of first-degree murder have histories of child abuse (*U.S. Department of Justice*, 2001). Prostitutes and juvenile delinquents also report histories of child abuse (Ibid.).

Society is wounded by an unimaginable number of individuals walking around who are suffering from various forms of pathological disorders due to such abuse.

When first investigating the issue of child abuse, one is tempted to say that our modern society is experiencing an epidemic of child abuse. In terms of sexual child abuse, it is reported that 1,100 children are abused every day, 400,000 every year. In our society, one in four girls, and one in seven boys are sexually abused before the age of eighteen. Fifty to seventy percent of sexual abuse is perpetuated on children by neighbors, friends and acquaintances. Thirty to fifty percent of sexual abuse is perpetuated on children by parents and relatives (*National Center on Child Abuse and Neglect*, 2001).

Sexual abuse of children cuts across all boundaries. One's economic level, race, ethnic heritage and religious faith have no bearing on the sexual abuse of children. Parents, relatives, teachers, priests, ministers, rabbis are all part of the tragedy of sexual abuse.

When the dignity due to every person is not taken seriously then evil is bound to follow. When one fails to recognize life at its first moments, at conception, then is it so much a surprise that the dignity of persons can be assaulted? Child abuse is a direct attack on the individual's dignity as a child of God. It is a direct attack on a child who is the "image and likeness of God.".

May society always remember the words of Christ who reminded all that whoever harms a "little one" will have to pay a great price, for as he said: "It would be better for a person to have a millstone put around his neck and be thrown into the sea than to harm a little one" (Lk. 17:2).

Those in society who violate the boundaries of sacredness are called to turn themselves into the proper authorities, enter into treatment, seek God's forgiveness, and do acts of penance and reparation.

XX
Modern Comprehensive Sex Education

"Sexual science is of two kinds, that which is used for controlling or overcoming the sexual passion, and that which is used to stimulate and feed it. Instruction in the former is as necessary a part of a child's education, as the latter is harmful and dangerous, and fit, therefore, only to be shunned. The sex education that I stand for must have for its object the conquest and sublimation of the sex passion. Such education should automatically serve to bring home to children the essential distinction between man and brute, to make them realize that it is man's special privilege and pride to be gifted with the faculties of head and heart both, that he is a thinking no less than feeling animal, and to renounce the sovereignty of reason over the blind instincts is, therefore, to renounce a man's estate. In man, reason quickens and guides the feeling; in brutes, the soul lies ever dormant."

Gandhi, Wisdom for All Times:
Mahatma Gandhi and Pope Paul VI
on Birth Regulation

The sex education programs found in schools today have left the world a legacy of sexual brutes, fostering large masses of individuals, if not an entire generation, incapable of authentically loving.

There are essentially three types of sex education programs competing for acceptance in our culture. One is referred to as chastity education, another as biological sex education, and a final as comprehensive sex education.

Chastity Sex Education

Chastity sex education is that which recognizes the uniqueness of individuals and fosters authentic sexual integrity and authentic love. It fosters self-mastery and the most intimate nature of the human person. It is only through chastity sex education that one can experience real love and the gifts that flow from fidelity.

The reality is that one either controls one's sexual drive or one is controlled by it. As the 1995 Vatican document *The Truth and Meaning of Human Sexuality* states:

> *"If the person is not the master of self— through the virtues and, in a concrete way, through chastity—he or she lacks that self-possession which makes self-giving possible. Chastity is the spiritual power which frees love from selfishness and aggression... Chastity is the joyous affirmation of someone who knows how to live self-giving, free from any form of self-centered slavery... Either man governs his passions and finds peace, or he lets himself be dominated by them and becomes unhappy"* (16, 17, 18).

> *"Chastity is not to be understood as a re-pressive attitude. On the contrary, chastity should be understood rather as the purity and temporary stewardship of a precious and rich gift of love, in view of the self-giving realized in each person's specific vocation. Chastity is thus the spiritual energy capable of defending love from the perils of selfishness and aggressiveness, and is able to advance it toward its full realization"* (14).

Those who cannot master chastity will never be able to master fidelity and authentic self-giving, for they will be slaves to their passions. They will never grasp the meaning of authentic family life, of authentic love and virtue and the respect for God's gift of sexuality and life. They will never be able to understand the intrinsic spirituality of the sex act.

The consequences of failing to foster chastity and self-mastery is the relinquishing of one's sexual energies to one's uncontrolled passions. This leads to the use of contraceptives (including abortifacients), divorce, abortion, child abuse, and perversions of all kinds. It leads to the disintegration between the body and soul, the physical and the spiritual.

Biological and Comprehensive Sex Education

Biological sex education focuses on the purely biological functioning of the reproductive system with no regard to the spiritual. It is secular and atheistic or agnostic in approach.

Closely related to this, is the more hideous form of sex education known as comprehensive sex education. This has become the leading sex education program in the public schools.

Building upon the purely biological, the comprehensive sex education program's philosophy is essentially as follows: "If it is between two consenting adults, it is acceptable." There is no right or wrong. There is no moral value system. There is no spiritual dimension to the person. There is no interest in interpersonal relationships or chastity skills. The person is an organism, like any other. One is an animal like any other, and thus one can for all practical purposes act like any other animal.

This is the philosophy that has conquered our culture and our school systems. Public school textbooks teach premarital sex, open marriages or free unions, group sex, homosexuality, bisexuality, sadomasochism, incest, bestiality, masturbation, sex with inanimate objects, etc.--all discussed without any moral significance. Birth control, abortion, sterilization, and so forth, are discussed without any value attached to them.

This philosophy says, "No sex act is immoral. No lifestyle must be judged."

What has this philosophy done to our culture? (cf. Clowes, *Facts of Life; Bureau of Census; Statistical Abstract; Index of Leading Cultural Indicators*)

- Despite the pushing of contraceptives, abortions have increased from 200,000 to between 1.1 and 1.4 million per year since 1960.
- Cohabitation has increased from 500,000 to 4 million.

- Divorce has increased from 400,000 to 1.2 million per year.
- Single-parent families have risen from 9 to 32 percent.
- Illegitimate births have increased from 200,000 to 1.5 million per year.
- Teenage pregnancy has increased from 30 to 110 per 1000 girls annually.
- Sexually transmitted diseases have increased 245 percent since 1960.
- Child abuse has increased 286 percents since 1960.
- Crime rates have increased by 510 percent.

When sex is divorced from its spiritual dimension, it lowers the person to the level of the brute, the animal. One either controls one's sexual drive or one is controlled by it!

"In man, reason quickens and guides the feeling;
in brutes, the soul lies ever dormant."
Gandhi

XXI
Premarital Sex

It is quite popular in today's secular culture to accept the popular message by educators, healthcare professionals, politicians, entertainers, and those in the media that premarital sex is harmless. The denial of essences, of the natural law, of the unitive and bonding nature of sex, of the nature of woman and man, and of absolutes has denigrated sex to its most base instincts. Is it any wonder that fifty percent of students that graduate from high school will have had premarital sex? Is it any wonder that seventeen percent of children in the seventh or eighth grade report having had sex? One in nine become pregnant! (CCC 1755, 1852, 2353: Cf. The Surgeon General's Call to Action to Promote Sexual Health, 2001).

Premarital sex has given rise to an epidemic of sexually transmitted diseases, an epidemic number of abortions, and the ever increasing rise in divorce rates. One point three million new cases of gonorrhea occur every year, with some strains being resistant to penicillin. According to the Center for Disease Control sixty-five million Americans are plagued with an incurable form of a sexually transmitted disease (CDC, 2005). It is estimated that every year some 60,000 to 100,000 young women are made sterile by HIV, gonorrhea or chlamydia. As many as a third of sexually active teenagers have genital warts. Sexually transmitted diseases infect approximately twelve million Americans each year. Two-thirds of sexually transmitted diseases occur in persons younger than twenty-five and every year more than three million teenagers are infected. This epidemic has caused many women to have problems with infertility—STD's being the fastest growing cause of infertility (The Surgeon General's Call to Action to Promote Sexual Health, 2001). It is estimated that one out of four adults have an STD (Center for Disease Control and Prevention, November 2007).

The epidemic in infections caused by premarital sex has led to the secular mirage of safe sex. The CDC refers to safe sex as oral sex, mutual masturbation, and sex with a condom—and if safe sex fails then abortion or the morning after pill, the morning after abortion is waiting. Each year 400,000 young women under twenty will have an abortion, and within a year after their pregnancy, one in five will become pregnant again and seek another abortion. Nearly one-half of all pregnancies are unintended (Ibid.).

Finally, premarital sex increases the divorce rate. Men have an innate desire to marry a virgin. Men who know that their wives have had a long sex life prior to marriage have a tendency of viewing their wives, whether consciously or unconsciously, as impure or even loose.

Statistics point to people engaged in premarital sex as having an increase in emotional and psychological problems, an increase in marital difficulties, and a proneness to engage in high-risk behavior detrimental to family and marital life (cf. CDC, 205).

XXII
Pornography

The misuse of sexuality is one of the most detrimental dimensions of the religion of secularism--and this is exemplified in a pornographic infested society.   Pornography is society's number one money making industry. It is sold everywhere, seen everywhere, and is thriving in leaps and bounds as the world goes deeper into the empty abyss of secularism.

Sex in the secular perspective is seen in terms of self-pleasuring and usefulness. It is devoid of all spiritual purpose and is completely alien to the very nature of conjugal love and the nature of the person. A person's sexuality in the secular vision of things has been distorted by its philosophies of pragmaticism, egoism, hedonism, positivism, and relativism, to name but a few.

A Catholic document titled *Human Sexuality* poignantly explains the damage that this secular pornographic contaminated society inflicts on individuals, marriages, children, and society in general.

"Pornography, the use of visual or print media to present nudity and sexual activity in a degrading or depersonalizing way, often preys upon the most vulnerable in our society. Women, children, and men all too often are portrayed as objects at the disposal of the sexual lust or violent actions of others.

> *Children, too, can find ready access to ma-*
> *terials that may warp their view of women*
> *and men, of sexuality, and of the mutual*
> *love and responsibility that rightly ought to*
> *accompany sexual intimacy (63)."*

Pornography distorts the purpose of sexuality and affronts human dignity. It eliminates from the essence of sex the mutual vulnerability that makes human intimacy possible. Pornography replaces vulnerability for control, power, and the objectification of the person. Pornography makes a mockery of the rights of spouses, of the institution of marriage, and compromises the welfare of children who need a healthy two parent home for stability.

Is it any wonder that adultery and marital infidelity are at epidemic levels? Is it any wonder that promiscuity has reached levels unheard of since the time of paganism? Is there any wonder that prostitution is rampant and has even gained a sense of legitimacy? Is it any wonder that a study by Neil Malamuth of UCLA reported that 50% of men would have no problem raping a woman if they could be assured of getting away with it (Philadelphia Inquirer, Jan. 9, 1987)? Is it any wonder that ten year olds are sexually active and that twelve year olds are getting pregnant and having abortions? Is it any wonder that once the "spice of sex" is lost in a marriage, the marriage ends? Is it any wonder that rape, sexual assaults and child abuse have reached epidemic proportions? When one debases oneself to the level of a brute animal, one cannot but help act like a brute animal!

XXIII
Preferential Option for the Poor

*"It is a poverty to decide that a child must die
so that you may live as you wish."*
Blessed Mother Teresa of Calcutta

What Mother Teresa has said about abortion can very well be said about the hungry, the poor and the homeless around the world.

It is so easy for us to harden our hearts to the plight of the less fortunate (cf. Ps. 95). Yet the Gospel and the *Catechism of the Catholic Church* continue to remind us of the need to love our neighbor, and to have a preferential option or love for the poor (CCC 2448; *Libertatis conscientia*, 68).

In the United States, on any given day, four million children under the age of twelve and twenty-seven million adults go to bed hungry. On any given night, 500,000 to 700,000 people in the richest country in the world are homeless. Forty-four million lack healthcare insurance (U.S. Bureaus of Census; CCHIP).

In terms of world statistics, 30,000 to 40,000 people die of hunger every day. One in ten children dies before the age of five from malnutrition. Eight hundred million suffer malnutrition every day. Over 30,000 children die every day from preventable diseases such as diarrhea, malaria or from poor sanitary conditions. One hundred million people are homeless in the world. Eight hundred and eighty-eight million lack healthcare. The wealthiest fifth of the world's population consumes an astonishingly eighty-six percent of all goods and services, while the poorest fifth consumes one percent (UNICEF; Food for the Hungry; Food and Agriculture Organization of the United States).

Helping the needy is not as much an act of charity as it is a demand for justice (CCC 2446). It is an act of justice that has always been part of the Church's teachings (cf. Mt. 25:31-46; 5:42; 6:2-4; 8:20; 10:8; Lk. 6:20-22; Mk. 12:41-44; Jas. 2:13-16; 5:1-6; Eph. 4:28; cf. 1 Jn. 3:17). As St. John Chrysostom (d. 407) explains: "Not to enable the needy to share in our goods is to steal from them and deprive them of life (*Hom. In Lazaro*, 2,5: PG 48, 992). Blessings are to be shared.

Isolation is not part of Catholic tradition or spirituality. Christ calls us to be his ears, his eyes, his hands, his feet, and his voice in a world crying for him.

The Church, the body of Christ, demands us to build a world where a solidarity of nations can be established to eliminate hunger, poverty, and homelessness (CCC 2438). It demands of us that we aid in the moral, cultural, and economic development of countries (CCC 2438; 2440). This is a grave and unavoidable responsibility for the wealthiest nations (CCC 2439). This is a grave and unavoidable responsibility for each and every one of us who call ourselves Christian: "How can God's love survive in a man who has enough of this world's goods yet closes his heart to his brother when he sees him in need" (1 Jn. 3:17)? May the Lord have mercy on our souls if we remain silent and inactive.

XXIV
Healthcare:
A Basic Right

My father died in 1980, next to his car, in the streets of Los Angeles at the young age of fifty-two from a massive heart attack. The sad reality is that he did not have to die in this manner. My father was the victim of a healthcare system that is too often profit-oriented as opposed to person-oriented. He died because he was unable to find health insurance coverage for a pre-existing heart condition.

He needed heart bypass surgery, but no insurance company would insure him.

I wish this were an unusual case.

Unfortunately, I have seen too many people die or become seriously ill unnecessarily because of a lack of health insurance or poor health insurance coverage.

In the year 2000 it was reported that 8.5 million children and 39.3 million adults were without health insurance (U.S. Census Bureau).

In the wealthiest nation the world has ever seen, this is not acceptable. The providing of healthcare to all citizens in the United States is a basic requirement of a civilized society (CCC 2288). Pope John Paul II in his encyclical letter Laborem Exercens reminds the nations of the world that healthcare "should be easily available for people and that as far as possible it should be cheap or even free of charge" (19:5).

The bishops of the United States powerfully remind us of our call as Christians when they state: "In a world characterized by growing prosperity for some and pervasive poverty for others, Catholic teaching proclaims that a basic moral test is how our most vulnerable members are faring. In a society marred by deepening divisions between rich and poor, our tradition recalls the story of the Last Judgment (Mt. 25:31-46) and instructs us to put the needs of the poor vulnerable first" (USCCB, Social Development and World Peace).

How are our most vulnerable members without healthcare faring? What can we do to help?

[Enlightened societies must be prudential in their offering of universal healthcare. What is being offered must indeed be healthcare. In recent years, abortion, the dispensing of abortifacient contraceptives, and euthanasia have been defined as healthcare. Aborting human life, either through direct abortion or the use of abortifacients, and the ending of life prematurely can never be seen as healthcare. Healthcare is based on the Hippocratic Oath: "I will not give a lethal drug to anyone if I am asked, nor will I advise such a plan; and similarly I will not give a woman a pessary to cause an abortion."]

XXV
Overpopulation:
An Evil Myth

The idea that the world is overpopulated is a myth that the wealthy nations of the world and those with pro-abortion and pro-contraceptive agendas seek to promote. The wealthy nations seek to keep their standard of living up at the cost of the poor: the wealthiest fifth of the world's population consumes astonishingly eighty-six percent of all the goods and services, while the poorest fifth consumes one percent, according to UNICEF.

The pharmaceutical companies and Planned Parenthood, the world's leading abortion provider, have tremendous profits at stake in promoting the overpopulation myth. Their agenda is quite simple: contraception, abortion, sterilization. When one worships the god of money, innocents die!

Let us look at the real facts. If you took the entire population of the world, you could fit it comfortably into the state of Texas, with no greater population density than New Jersey. According to the U.S. Printing Office the world population in the year 2001 was 6.15 billion with a growth rate of .02 percent. Since 1900, food production has exceeded population increases. According to the United Nations' Population Information Network, the world's population will grow to 7.3 billion by the year 2040 and then level off.

While it is true that the population in so-called

"third world" countries is increasing, the population in many countries in so-called "first world" countries is on the decline. In most European nations, the birth rate does not equal the death rate, thus failing to even reach the level of replacement.

The fact that the world's population is in no danger of overpopulating the earth or in over-consuming the world's resources, does not mean that everything is okay.

Much of the population control being done in the world is not through Natural Family Planning and economic and industrial development, but through the evil means of abortion, sterilization, and contraception.

Furthermore, when we look below the surface of the distribution of resources in the world, we see a great imbalance, which leads to grave injustices. We see that 30,000 to 40,000 people die of hunger every day. One in ten children dies before the age of five from malnutrition. Eight hundred million suffer malnutrition every day. Over 30,000 children die every day from preventable diseases such as diarrhea, malaria, or from poor sanitary conditions. One hundred million people are homeless in the world. Eight hundred and eighty million lack healthcare.

In the name of combating hunger and population control, people who support abortion, contraception and sterilization are people that often misunderstand the poorest of the poor. Couples in the so-called "third world" have large families (i.e., five or more children) not out of ignorance but out of necessity. In the West we have social security and a pension plan when we retire. In the "third world" social security is found not in a check but in a couple's children. Since—on average--one out of ten children die before the age of five in these poorest of poor countries, a couple's only means of survival into old age (when they can no longer work the fields, etc.) is to have children to take care of them. The more children one has the greater chance that some will survive to take care of them.

The wealthy countries must be willing to help in the development of the less fortunate nations, and they must be willing to share their excess of resources. As was mentioned before, the wealthiest fifth of the world's population consumes astonishingly eighty-six percent of all the goods and services, while the poorest fifth consumes one percent, according to UNICEF. A more generous heart is needed, even if our standard of living decreases. As Mother Teresa of Calcutta said: "It is a poverty to decide that a child must die so that we may live as we wish."

What then is the answer? When Margaret Sanger, the founder of Planned Parenthood, attempted to introduce contraceptives into India, Mahatma Gandhi reprimanded Sanger by pointing to the reality that what India needed was not contraceptives but "the proper land system, better agriculture and supplementary industry." If this was done, Gandhi continued, "India would be capable of supporting twice as many people."

The Holy Father, John Paul II, in his work *Evangelium Vitae*, summed up the Catholic teaching on population management and authentic development: "Governments and various national agencies must above all strive to create economic, social, public health and cultural conditions which will enable married couples to make their choices about procreation in full freedom and with genuine responsibility (i.e., using natural family planning). They must make efforts to ensure greater opportunities and a fairer distribution of wealth so that everyone can share equitably in the goods of creation. Solutions must be sought on the global level by establishing a true economy of communion and sharing of goods, in both the national and international order. This is the only way to respect the dignity of persons and families, as well as the authentic cultural patrimony of peoples" (91).

XXVI
Economic Justice

Christians are called to a communion of persons, in imitation of our God. Because of this call, one is held to the demands of justice and peace in conformity with right-reason and divine wisdom (CCC 2419). One is called to defend the dignity of the person as the image and likeness of his or her maker.

The Church is obligated to make judgments on economic and social matters when the souls of individuals are at stake. All aspects of life in the social and economic dimension are to be ordered to the eternal destiny of people.

The following points are central to Catholic social justice:

• "Any system in which social relationships are determined entirely by economic factors is contrary to the nature of the human person and his acts" (CA, 35).

• "A theory that makes profit the exclusive norm and ultimate end of economic activity is morally unacceptable. The disordered desire for money cannot but produce perverse effects. It is one of the causes of the many conflicts which disturb the social order" (GS 63,3; LE 7; 20; CA 35).

• "A system that subordinates the basic rights of individuals and of groups to the collective organization of production is contrary to human dignity. Every practice that reduces persons to nothing more than a means of profit enslaves man, leads to idolizing money, and contributes to the spread of atheism. You cannot serve God and mammon" (GS 65, 2; Mt. 6:24; Lk. 16:13).

• "The Church has rejected the totalitarian and atheistic ideologies associated in modern times with communism or socialism. She has likewise refused to accept, in the practice of capitalism, individualism and the absolute primacy of the law of the marketplace over human labor. Regulating the economy solely by centralized planning perverts the basis of social bonds; regulating it solely by the law of the marketplace fails social justice, for there are many human needs which cannot be satisfied by the market. Reasonable regulation of the marketplace and economic initiatives, in keeping with a just hierarchy of values and a view to the common good, is to be commended" (CA 10; 13; 34; 44).

The rich nations have a responsibility for the poorer nations in a spirit of solidarity and charity.

XXVII
Workers' Rights

Providing for the needs of workers is a fundamental right in all civilizations. Providing for the needs of workers must be in accordance to the moral law and right reason.

Work is a duty (cf. 1 Thess. 4:11; 2 Thess. 3:10) that honors the Creator and by its nature should be redemptive (cf. Gen. 3:14-19) and directed toward the salvation of the person.

Workers' rights should include the following (cf. CCC 2426f):

1. Workers have the right to employment.

2. Workers have the right to a sufficient and just wage to provide for the material, social, cultural and spiritual welfare of one's life, one's family, and the common good of one's community.

3. The good of workers must not be infringed upon at the expense of profit.

4. All workers have a right to employment without discrimination.

5. Conflicts should be resolved by just negotiation with the dignity of all involved respected. In the event of an impasse, the right to strike for a proportionate benefit

must be assured. Violence, however, is not
to be resorted to.
6.   A worker has the right to social security benefits, public services (i.e., healthcare), and freedom of movement in jobs.

Providing for the needs of workers is a fundamental right in all civilizations. Providing for the needs
of workers must be in accordance with the moral law and
right reason.

XXVIII
Concluding Remarks

The theologian Jules Girardi, in summarizing why so many fail to believe in Christ, explained, "The scandal of 'believers' is not chiefly that of some crime or other, rather it is that Christianity does not startle the world."

Gandhi once mentioned that he never became a Christian because he never met one.

While we clearly find flaws in such statements, and rightly so, we must however ask ourselves whether we are doing our part to startle the world? Are we making our presence known?

The existentialist philosopher Albert Camus, while standing over the crushed body of a young boy, turned to his friend and said while pointing to the sky: "You see, the sky is dumb."

Are we there to answer a Camus? Are we there to point to the way, the truth, and the life?

The Jesuit theologian Karl Rahner once said: "The devout Christian of the future will either be a 'mystic,' one who has 'experienced' something, or he will cease to be anything at all." We as Christians are called to be different, to be recognizably different. May no one mistake who we are.

When we look to the media, we see so much confusion in the world. We see the Gospel values being undermined in subtle and often overt ways. We see a world that is becoming more and more foreign to the Gospel message. We see violence and injustices of all kinds—

abortion, euthanasia, cloning, embryonic stem cell research, racism, prejudice, promiscuity, and so forth. The world is crying for Christ, crying for authentic love, crying for a direction in life. We see a world in so much need of healing.

To be a Christian today is not an easy task. But just as we wave the American flag around, we must wave the Christian flag around.

We must make our presence known. Just as we are not afraid to be known as Americans, we must not be afraid to be known as Catholics. Just as we are willing to die for our country, we must be willing to die for our faith!

We live in a world we are fully aware of, a world with many distinct visions of reality, and we recognize that one way or another we will accept one vision of reality. It is inescapable. What lenses will we wear? The lenses we wear will influence our understanding of reality and our response to reality.

May we always renew our commitment to see the world through the lenses, the eyes, of Christ. To do such is to see reality the way it authentically is.

Let us seek to recognize that God sees his Son in each and every one of us; that we are created in his image and likeness; and that we bear the handprint of God in our very being. If we can do so, we will truly startle the world for Christ. We will startle the world for the Gospel of Life.

Also available from
Fr. John J. Pasquini
and Vero House Publishing:

CATHOLIC ANSWERS TO PROTESTANT QUESTIONS

A CONCISE SUMMARY

www.VeroHousePublishing.com

CPSIA information can be obtained at www.ICGtesting.com
Printed in the USA
LVOW130242190313

324896LV00001B/1/P